EYE TO EYE WITH DOGS

YORKSHIRE TERRIERS

Lynn M. Stone

Rourke
Publishing LLC
Vero Beach, Florida 32964

www.rourkepublishing.com

PHOTO CREDITS: All photos © Lynn M. Stone

Title page: *Always ready to play, a Yorkshire Terrier waits for game time to begin.*

Acknowledgments: For their help in the preparation of this book, the author thanks Arlene King, Roberta Rothenbach, and Debbie Tabor.

Editor: Frank Sloan

Cover and page design by Nicola Stratford

Library of Congress Cataloging-in-Publication Data

Stone, Lynn M.
  Yorkshire terriers / Lynn M. Stone.
    p. cm. -- (Eye to eye with dogs II)
  Includes bibliographical references and index.
  ISBN 1-59515-163-X (hardcover)
  1. Yorkshire terrier--Juvenile literature. I. Title. II. Series: Stone, Lynn M. Eye to eye with dogs II.
  SF429.Y6S76 2004
  636.76--dc22

                                                                    2004008019

Printed in the USA

CG/CG

Table of Contents

The Yorkie's long, silky coat is its trademark.

The Yorkshire Terrier

The Yorkshire terrier is one of the "toy" dog **breeds**. Being one of the toy breeds simply means that a dog is lap-sized. But a Yorkie almost looks like a very fancy toy with its dark, button-sized eyes and nose.

YORKSHIRE TERRIER FACTS	
Weight:	Not more than 7 pounds (3 kilograms)
Height:	8-9 inches (21-23 centimeters)
Country of Origin:	England
Life Span:	14-16 years

Perhaps no other breed, for its size, has a coat as long and silky as the Yorkie.

The Yorkshire terrier's coat has helped make it a favorite breed of people who like small, long-haired dogs.

A Yorkshire terrier looks like a furry toy.

The Yorkshire looks fancy, but it's a perky, fun-loving breed.

A Yorkie dashes through a tube in an agility trial event.

But if a Yorkie looks fancy, it doesn't act that way. These little dogs, like many other terriers, were developed to find, attack, and kill rats. People don't choose Yorkies for their rat-catching ability any longer. But modern Yorkies still have the energy and courage of their **ancestors**.

A Yorkie sails through a plastic ring during agility training.

The Dog for You?

Yorkies are friendly and playful dogs. They love games, and they like to fetch. Anyone who owns a Yorkie should be willing to play games with the dog.

Careful grooming makes a Yorkie's long hair lie flat and shiny.

The Yorkie's red hair bow keeps hair out of its eyes.

Yorkshire terriers are so independent that they aren't always easy to teach. However, they can be taught **obedience** and even **agility** by a patient owner.

Yorkies on-leash like a short hike, but as a rule they are not outdoor dogs. They are small enough to get good exercise just by romping in the home.

Many Yorkie owners show their dogs. Yorkshire terriers with ribbons on their foreheads and finely combed body fur are ready for the show ring.

Yorkies with long fur need combing or brushing almost every day. People who don't show their Yorkshire terriers often trim their fur, especially during the warm months.

Despite their small size, Yorkshire terriers make good watchdogs.

Like other terriers, Yorkies are quick to bark at strangers.

Many Yorkies have their hair trimmed for easier grooming and summertime comfort.

A Yorkie plays in leaves. Early Yorkies were rough-and-tumble outdoor dogs.

Sometimes Yorkies act like they have no idea how small they are. They can be **aggressive** toward other dogs.

And just because Yorkshire terriers are small doesn't mean they should be left alone with small children.

Yorkshire Terriers of the Past

The Yorkshire terrier's roots are not in fancy grooming and show rings. Instead, people in Yorkshire, England, developed the Yorkie in the 1800s as a **ratter**.

They **crossed** several breeds of terriers, probably including the waterside, Clydesdale, and Maltese, among others.

The waterside terrier was probably a major ancestor of the Yorkie. A Scottish dog, the waterside was a small, blue-gray terrier with fairly long hair.

Crossing with other terriers led to the modern Yorkshire terrier.

The Yorkies' long hair made them a standout among terriers.

No one knows if the English were *trying* to develop an especially beautiful terrier. But that is what they got. By the late 1800s, Yorkshire terriers were being shown by wealthy owners in England and America.

Many of the early Yorkies weighed between 12 and 14 pounds (5 and 6 kg). Yorkie owners decided they preferred smaller dogs, so they began choosing only smaller Yorkies to be parent dogs. Today's Yorkshire terriers are not supposed to weigh more than 7 pounds (3 kg).

Yorkies are the most popular terriers on the planet.

Wearing a robe of fur, a Yorkie waits to be combed.

The American Kennel Club accepted the Yorkshire terrier onto its list of official breeds in 1885. Today the Yorkie is the most popular terrier in the world.

Looks

A Yorkshire terrier with a full, combed coat looks like a bit like it's wearing a robe. Its long fur reaches from its back to the ground, hiding the dog's legs and its tail. Its muzzle hair is combed in a wide, drooping mustache. The forehead ribbon locks up long fur that would otherwise cover the dog's eyes.

Yorkie pups are born black and tan. As they age, they gain the adult colors of tan and shades of gray, usually described as "blue."

Yorkie pups take a break from mom.

A Note about Dogs

Puppies are cute and cuddly, but only after serious thought should anybody buy one. Puppies grow up.

And remember that a dog will require more than love and patience. It will need healthy food, exercise, grooming, a warm, safe place in which to live, and medical care.

A dog can be your best friend, but you need to be its best friend, too.

Choosing the right breed requires some homework. For more information about buying and owning a dog, contact the American Kennel Club at http://www.akc.org/index.cfm or the Canadian Kennel Club at http://www.ckc.ca/.

Glossary

agility (uh JIL u tee) — the ability to perform certain athletic tasks, such as leaping through a hoop

aggressive (eh GRES iv) — wanting to attack or attacking

ancestor (AN SES tur) — an animal that at some past time was part of the modern animal's family

breeds (BREEDZ) — particular kinds of domestic animals within a larger, closely related group, such as the Yorkshire terrier breed within the dog group

crossed (KROSSD) — to have been mated with an animal of a different breed

obedience (o BEED ee unts) — the willingness to follow someone's direction or command; a pre-set training program for dogs

ratter (RAT ur) — a dog developed and used mostly for finding and killing rats

Index

Further Reading

Carroll, David L. *The ASPCA Complete Guide to Pet Care.* Plume, 2001

Downing, Elisabeth. *Guide to Owning a Yorkshire Terrier.*
    Chelsea House, 1999

Fogle, Bruce. *The Dog Owner's Manual.* DK Publishing, 2003

Website to Visit

Yorkshire Terrier Club of America at www.ytca.org

About the Author

Lynn M. Stone is the author of more than 400 children's books. He is a talented natural history photographer as well. Lynn, a former teacher, travels worldwide to photograph wildlife in its natural habitat.